DEDICATION

This book is dedicated to all of the women and men who are tired of going through the motions and living an unfulfilled life. I hope you will find some inspiration in the following pages to take the reins and ride off into the sunset of your best chapter yet!

I also want to thank all of the horses who have shown up in my life to act as some of my most profound teachers.

HAPPY TRAILS!

A SPECIAL THANKS

I would like to acknowledge the women in my close circle or as I call them, my First-Class Cabin. These ladies were my cheerleaders as I stepped into the unknown of transforming my life and then encouraging me to write a book about it!

The woman who has priority boarding with her name engraved on a seat is Susan F. Moody. Susan is a brilliant businesswoman with a genuine heart of gold. We have navigated a few journeys together and I know there are more in our future. I have learned such strength, resilience, and grace through our connection, and without it, I never would have even considered compiling my journey into a book.

I appreciate you every day Susan, and am grateful for our friendship and all of the help and support with this book and yes, sometimes talking me off the ledge as only you can do.

UNBRIDLE IT!

Buck Up and Create Your Happy!

Leeanne Gardner

UNBRIDLE IT

Library of Congress Control Number: 2021901188

ISBN: 978-1-7363890-0-3

First Printing: January 2021

Published by: Leeanne Gardner
Cave Creek, AZ

UNBRIDLE

CONTENTS

"What's Your It?"

After almost 25 years working in corporate offices of airlines, software development companies, and luxury hotels, I found myself facing a layoff in 2008 as I chose not to relocate from Scottsdale, AZ to New York City. Something inside of me had made the decision that it was no longer about titles and money that come with the corporate life; it was about how could I make a difference.

Oh yeah, and this was about a year after I had decided to leave an 11-year marriage (Yippee skippee for me, no stress going on there...I learned to like red wine...a lot!) On a Southwest flight to NYC while still employed in 2008, I opened the magazine to an article about a ranch in Tucson, AZ, that was using horses to help women and corporate teams learn life lessons. This got my attention.

During the years I had horses at home, I had more intimately experienced their magic. After a long day at work, I would grab my adult beverage of choice and just go hang out with my little herd of horses. I would feel the stress leave my body, and my heart fill with love for these animals, so I knew there must be more to it. I was intrigued as I had long known the healing abilities of horses and how they were used for amazing partnerships with Autistic children and other developmentally disabled individuals. So began my journey into exploring how to partner with my horses, Romeo and Sassy, to help people learn to get out of their heads and reconnect with a passion. I would have discussions with my corporate colleagues and ask them about their passion or what lights them up, and they would just kind of look at me. So, I knew I was on to something. I wanted to help people find their passion!

This was important to me as once I had allowed myself to reconnect with the horses, I could speak to the importance of living with passion and life balance. As you will read later, this took 16 years to happen, after FINALLY letting down that wall I constructed due to the pain from the loss of my first horse. What I realized is that I was not alone, far from it.

Almost every person on the planet has lost something near and dear to them based on circumstances beyond their control. In my case, my first horse due to my parent's divorce. Other examples could be that you loved art or playing an instrument, and you were told you were horrible, so you allowed someone else to steal your joy.

Did you ever reconnect with that joy or experience that used to bring you happiness, or are you continuing to keep your distance? I will give you an example that may strike a chord:

I was a speaker at a Leadership Conference in 2015, and I was delivering my *"Unbridle Your Passion and Lead with Your Heart"* presentation. When we got to the Q&A, I posed the question to the audience; *"What passion have you walked away from because someone told you that you couldn't do it or weren't good enough?"* A woman in the audience started to tear up. I noticed and softly asked if she wanted to share.

She slowly started to talk about it. As a child, she loved to play the piano; it gave her joy. However, her father would tell her how bad she was, and one day the piano was just gone. My story about losing my horse struck a chord as she could relate to that pain of having something that was important and brought such joy taken away from her. I challenged her to go start to play the piano, and she did. Each time I would see her at a networking event, I would always ask if she was still playing, and she was.

You see, we give people such power when we listen to their negative comments, and I would venture to say that very few people ever allow themselves to go back and reconnect to "It." That is where my tag line originally came from, "What's your **It**?" What lights you up?

If this has struck a chord with something you have walked away from, good…that means that you have a chance to reconnect with IT, and in this book, I'll give you some steps so that you can Buck Up and Create Your Happy!

Ready to saddle up and join me?

~ *Leeanne*

Bucking Up!

"Step out of the history that is holding you back. Step into the new story you are willing to create." ~ Oprah Winfrey

When I first decided to write this book, it was at the encouragement of friends who had witnessed my complete transformation over a few months at the onset of the Coronavirus pandemic in the Spring of 2020. I thought of a clever title, "The 'Rona Reset," and set about to create a how-to book detailing how I was able to make positive changes in every area of my life during a pandemic! Believe me; it was empowering. However, as the months rolled on, I felt that there was so much more to my "sudden" transformation and decided to reflect on that.

It struck me that up until this point in my life, I had not accumulated all the tools that would help me SUCCESSFULLY make all of these positive changes. Maybe I had not walked through some of these life lessons, or maybe I had, yet I had not learned them until the ripe age of 55. What I also realized through my journey of building my resilience muscles was that so many of the lessons I learned were through my love affair with horses. From the loss of my first love, a horse, at a young age and the subsequent reconnection with horses 16 years later, I was able to learn valuable life lessons that I live by. I am so passionate about helping others understand how horses are some of our best teachers and allowing them to experience this horse-human connection firsthand.

So, this transformation was not sudden at all; it was the culmination of my life experiences and the determination to take the reins of my own life and get back on track with my purpose. Only this time, with more tools and experience. It worked, and I continue to follow my steps each day. I hope that you can find some valuable tips to incorporate into your own journey.

I knew something had to change and that it all started with me. It was time that I listened to my own advice and ask, "What lights you up? What's your IT?" So, this is where it all begins. I decided to take the reins and create the life that I was meant to live.

When the first hints of the Coronavirus pandemic hit about March 2020, and the panic for small business owners started to increase, something inside of me was energized. I know. I am a little crazy that way as I do not follow the crowd that feeds off drama and doom and gloom. Instead, I try to look for the positives and opportunities amidst the chaos. I saw this whole situation as a major opportunity for people to regroup and reset. The changes that I made positively affected both my personal life and, as a solopreneur, my business. I will share some basic tools that I used to be able to make some significant positive changes in 90 days, and the changes are continuing as I have now adopted these tools as daily practices.

I decided to make some major changes for MYSELF. At the time, I did not have a plan; I just knew that the life I was living was not working for me, and I felt stuck. Looking back now and what encouraged me to write the book, in addition to my friends who witnessed my complete transformation, were the three areas that I was able to focus on and change.

1. Self-Care
2. Relationships
3. Alignment with My Purpose

In addition, I have been able to refer back to the new habits I created when I find myself falling back into old patterns.

So...truth be told...I am not a big book reader... SO WHY NOT WRITE A BOOK??? My intention for this book is that when you are in a funk or ready to make changes, you can pick it up, read a chapter and do some of the worksheets to get you back on track. You can do it all at once if you are a crazy overachiever like me or focus on one aspect at a time. This is not a one and done; it is truly a lifestyle change that I have committed to that continues to bring me amazing gifts and opportunities each day. Don't get me wrong, I still spin, but at the first signs of anxiety knocking on my door, I stop myself and follow my own steps. If I can do it, so can you! This really is about learning to tune in to your heart and get out of your head.

You CAN make these changes; you just need to tap into what exists inside of you and commit to doing the work. When I reflected on what actions I took, it really came down to 3 things in each case...and I am all about the Power of 3! These 3 are the same regardless of if you are seeking positive change in your personal or business life. But it ALL starts with YOU, personally, as if your personal foundation has a crack in it, chances are your business will be feeling the effects as well.

REASSESS (What's Not Working?)
Where are you today, in this moment? What is working and what is not? Are you satisfied, or do

you know there is more happiness and potential you just have not tapped into yet?

The first step I chose to take was to look at my life and ask myself some tough questions. I call this the "Reassess" phase, as by looking at the here and now, you can establish your baseline and then break each area down into areas to focus on. Each different aspect will most likely need its own plan of action in order to turn it around. And some will take longer than others. The key is that you first take the time to really figure out what is not working that you are ready to change.

REALIGN – (What Will Work and How Do I Get There?)
What is your passion? What lights you up? For Business, are you still on track with your "Why," or have you derailed?

Life sometimes takes us way down a path until we wake up one day and realize that this is not the path we want to be on. Until this reality hits, it does not faze us that we need to get back on track or re-aligned with our life's mission. Once you step into living your purpose and making a difference, you can achieve your life's mission to give back as only you can do. It's not about money and appearances. For me, it is about showing up authentically and making a difference for others that makes my heart happy. It isn't imperative that you know your passion or purpose, only that you give yourself permission to explore that which feels lighter, possibly remembering something from childhood that brought you joy.

REIGNITE – (How Will I Make it Work?) *Imagine how you will feel once you have made your desired changes.*

This is where your commitment comes in to do what it takes to make the changes necessary to embrace your next chapter. Once you have consistently adopted some of the practices I will offer in the coming pages, you will feel a sense of excitement and energy.

As you shift into a mindset, and possibly even a physical space, that is more aligned with your goals and ambitions, the people and opportunities will start appearing.

Lessons Learned from the Horses

I began showing horses about age eight. Horse shows are a competition where you and your horse are judged in a variety of different classes. Some are judged on the horse's appearance and conformation, some are judged on how you maneuver through a series of obstacles or a pattern with precision (that was my favorite), and some are judged on the partnership between you and the horse. "Judged," yes, very judgmental, and sometimes political; however, when we translate this into life, it is all about showing up and doing the best you can every day. If you never put yourself in the arena, you will never know how far you can go or what you can achieve. Win or lose; you need to show up, do your best, and have fun!

Are you ready to Buck Up and Unbridle It?! You will thank yourself for it.

American Royal Horse Show with my first love Dooby, 1980.

Let's Get To IT!

B - *Be Honest* – What's Not Working?

U - *Unapologetically You* – This is YOUR life, don't compare your journey to anyone else. What needs to change to help YOU create a more fulfilled life? Why is it important that you make this change?

C - *Claim Desired Outcome* – Imagine how you will feel once you have embraced the positive changes. How will this affect your life?

K - *Kick It into Gear* – Develop an action plan and get busy!

U - *Unbridle Your Passion* – Get excited about the new life you are creating!

P - *Put Yourself in the Arena* – You have done the work, and now it's time to confidently walk through the gate! You'll never know how far you can go unless you take that first step into the arena.

REASSESS

REALIGN

REIGNITE

Happiness is an Inside Job

"Action may not always bring happiness, but there is no happiness without action."
~ William James

We have all heard it before, but it is 100% true. You cannot find happiness externally until you find what makes you happy internally. It is up to you to spend some time figuring out what happiness looks and feels like to YOU. Too frequently we put too much emphasis on thinking it will come from a relationship. It starts and ends with you.

When you have found your happy, the people that are best aligned to help you with your new journey will appear. If you haven't taken the time to work on yourself, the same is true, people will show up to test you and until you do your own work to figure out your shit and what makes you happy, you will continue to attract the people that are not what you deserve.

Sometimes we think we will be happy when we achieve something...like when you achieve a goal you set such as losing weight, getting married or in a relationship, buying a new outfit, car, etc. But if you are not happy with that person in the mirror, nothing external will make it so. It takes work and trial and error. You may find temporary happiness, but most likely, until you figure out your own stuff, it will not last.

Authenticity comes into play here as well. Don't fake it til you make it! Show UP! Don't just go through the motions and put on a big smile because that's what you think you're supposed to do. I learned the beauty and importance of showing up authentically through working with horses as this is their natural state of being. If you show up with an agenda or not being authentic or your true self, they will call you out on it!

For me, especially at this stage of life being 55, I was extremely comfortable being myself and I preached it to anyone who would listen. I am very empathic and see through a lot of people's bull since I have a business that frequently requires me to be around or facilitate large groups of people. Oh yeah, well until March 2020 when we could no longer gather in groups.... but you get the idea.

It is so important that you focus on just showing up and being honest. And another reason for me to make these changes was that I was not being honest with myself in living a life that inspired me and in alignment with the work of helping others that I knew was my calling.

I realized in the Spring of 2020 that I was not happy, and it was no one's fault. There is no blame. I just needed to take the time and determine what it was going to take to figure my own shit out and create a life that I was excited to wake up to each day. ***On my own...this is key***. You must start with yourself.

The lockdown afforded me the ability, and everyone else on the planet, to be alone and sit in that aloneness. For me, being alone used to be extremely uncomfortable. I do not enjoy doing things by myself being the youngest of six kids. But this was different...I found myself enjoying my beautiful rental house all by myself with my little dog Lucy and I began to learn to slow everything down.

The 'Rona Reset

As I have mentioned, Spring of 2020, I was not happy with my life and had not been for a while. At the end of December 2019, I had Shingles, so my body was jumping on the bandwagon to remind me that it was time to make some changes! My body is great at stepping up and shutting down when I'm overly stressed and not listening.

I was grateful to have a full stable of clients (yes,

there will be LOTS of horse references) and a steady income, which is always a welcome state for an entrepreneur, but something was missing. I just felt like I was not living the life I was supposed to live and was not comfortable in my physical environment. I felt out of place physically, mentally, and spiritually. I was impatient with those around me and did not like the woman I saw in the mirror.

When I decide to make a change, it's go big or go home. I usually do not make one small modification, which would be perfectly fine, I change EVERYTHING! One of my first major shifts was in 1994 when I left a 10-year career with American Airlines, accepted a job in a place I had never been (Scottsdale, AZ), moved from a place I loved (Austin, TX), and got engaged (to a man that I had recently broken up with). I think I hit most of the major life events other than pregnancy and death with that one.

Early signs from the medical professionals indicated that some of the individuals most impacted by Covid-19 had some health issues associated with obesity. I saw it as a wake-up call. If people could focus on releasing some weight and getting healthier, then they would not only have many positive longer-term benefits but could also decrease their risk for the severe impacts caused by the virus. One of the most common excuses for people to put off self-care is not enough time. Well...we all had PLENTY of time when we were all forced to stay home due to the pandemic, so that excuse did not fly with me. I knew that I had been griping about my excess 20 lbs. and it was up to me to do something about it.

Many people were overcome with FEAR. FEAR brings up panic and a lot of people will reach for whatever will help comfort them and help them cope with the Fear of the unknown. Quite frequently, the go-to options selected are not the healthiest. Food, alcohol, and drugs are usually the top go-tos. Everyone needed to just find some sort of comfort in the complete unknown of what was happening all around us. Then, as people were giving themselves permission to eat and drink whatever to help them get through, they would share on social media and get support and found encouragement from others who were in the same boat of choosing unhealthy new habits.

Instead of buying into that fear-based victim thinking, I would just post positive and inspiring images on social media and quietly began my journey by taking advantage of the time to focus on getting healthier, which was the first step.

Where are you allowing your focus, time, and attention? Are you surrounded by the drama queens and kings who always see the negatives?

The people you surround yourself with have a tremendous impact on so many aspects of your life, both positive and negative.

Instead of feeling FEAR, I chose to see that feeling as excitement, a new start. A RESET. You have a choice when you interpret a feeling that bubbles up when you are faced with the unknown, Fear vs. Excitement. Think about that for a minute and how your mindset shifts when you are in both of these places. Fear will shut you down and bring up your defenses whereas Excitement opens you up to opportunities.

Can you feel the difference with that? This does not always work as sometimes the FEAR is real... like a bear is chasing you and your small dog. That is real. Ask yourself what is the worst that can happen when your fears pop up? If it is not a bear, or life-threatening, when we break it down, we take some power away from that fear that we have made up in our head.

What small step can you take today to address that Fear?

Sometimes, it is as simple as just taking a breath, or four, and visualizing a STOP sign which reminds you to shift before you sink into that doom loop. One step will lead to another step and the incremental progress will build and help you on your mission of conquering fears. Take the power away from the Fear.

Self-Care
Opportunity for a Physical and a Mental Reset

"It's not selfish to love yourself, take care of yourself, and to make your happiness a priority. It's necessary." ~ Mandy Hale

One definition of self-care that I resonate with is the fact that we first acknowledge the relationship we have with ourselves and prioritize it. This requires that we have to be intentional with our efforts to sustain our self-care. Sometimes we need to recognize that some of the things we are doing are not healthy for us and hold ourselves responsible. This one is an internal call to Buck Up!

Self-care is more than treating yourself to a massage, mani-pedi, or a workout. It encompasses your body, mind, and soul. In my opinion, your self-care should be a priority every day. If you are not in a good place, how do you expect to give your best to your personal or professional life? Overall wellness is one of the biggest contributors to your success in all aspects of your life.

For me, self-care is a necessity because when I get overstressed, my body revolts...it shuts me down. I mentioned I had Shingles for Christmas in 2019 (Thanks Santa!), in 2018 it was adrenal fatigue, and who could forget that fun two nights in Chicago Mercy Hospital stroke unit with heart attack symptoms in 2015 that was eventually diagnosed as "complex migraine" (with no head-aches). I started to listen after that one!

As we rolled into 2020, I was not comfortable with my body image and so one of my first goals was to learn to slow down, release some weight, and tap into the power of my intuition, my words, and my intentions. I felt out of place and unhappy physically, mentally, and spiritually.

Physical – Body

I have always been focused...well ok almost ob-sessed at times with my weight. For many years, I have gone up and down 10-15 pounds. I come from a family with several members who have struggled with their weight, so I knew I needed to be mindful as my genetics were predisposed for fuller figures. However, self-care is much more than losing weight, it's about who you are sur-rounding yourself with; what you are watching on the television, and social media; how you are talking to yourself; what thoughts you are allowing to take up space in your head; and, of course, the physical health aspects.

Choices, Choices

Instead of enjoying a daily glass of red wine, or maybe two, I chose not to have wine in the house during the week. I was committed to my new mission of getting healthy and releasing weight. Since all the gyms were closed, I started finding free workout videos on TV and extending my walks. So, no excuses that you do not have extra money as many options are all FREE!

For those people who are caregivers, healers, healthcare workers, etc., the work you do is so important, however, you must learn to focus your caregiving on yourself first. You are so busy taking care of everyone else, you have no energy left for yourself. This frequently leads to alcohol, tobacco, and food dependencies. If your purpose is to help and heal others, focus on giving them your best and most healthy self as an example for which to aspire.

Before the Spring of 2020, everyone had an excuse for not focusing on self-care, which was usually "time." Well, when the world came to a screeching halt, we all had nothing but time. That is what prompted me to get serious about my overall self-care from mindset to physical well-being and weight loss. So many people were on Facebook complaining about how they were gaining so much weight being home. For me, the weight was dropping off and the reason was my intentional focus on making positive changes to my self-care! But it was also the other mindset changes I was making to just slow everything down and focus on what it was that I wanted.

Weight loss

As I mentioned, I struggled with my weight most of my life, and since I am now over 50, just like you hear, it was more difficult for me to lose the excess baggage as they say. But I was determined AND committed. I used a new healthy lifestyle app and it helped me to learn how to make better choices that fit my lifestyle. For so long I thought going to the gym would counteract some happy hour beverages and too much Mexican food. Not so much.

With this program, I learned that my problem in the past was that I did not focus enough on the food part and now that I was, the weight started falling off. Find something that works for you that you can commit to. Whatever that may be, but nothing will work if you do not commit to it. I still follow the basics of this program today. What you eat and drink are major contributors to achieving and maintaining your desired and healthy weight.

If you want to release weight, then stop buying crap and having it in the house, do not fall for the gimmicks of a pill or shake, make better choices. It is all on you, sorry for the wake-up call, but it is!

I need structure and accountability and this app provided it along with some great psychology tips and coaching. As much or as little support as you need and it worked. Find something that works for YOU and you're more likely to stick with it!

Daily movement is necessary as well, but again, commit to something you will do! Do not go join a gym if you have never been a gym person! I walk (pretty fast) with the dogs, so not only do I get my exercise in, this is when I also get to appreciate the outdoors, desert beauty and can recite my daily gratitudes.

Living in Arizona, we have an abundance of beautiful desert hiking opportunities, again, these are FREE. If you have never hiked, do not try an advanced or challenging hike like Camelback for your first time out. Pick something enjoyable and reasonable for your fitness level. As with any new routine you wish to try, make it achievable or you will never stick with it. Find a friend or join a group of other like-minded individuals to explore and experience something new. I have returned to riding horses a couple of times per week, and continued my golf lessons. (I sound like a commercial for an active living community or Tampax!) Again, whatever method of exercise or movement works for you! The point is...get moving!

Physical – Living Space

Since I had made the decision to end the relationship and I was living in his house, I needed to find a place to move with WAAAY too many clothes and not so much furniture. I knew that my physical space needed to change closer to being with the horses. My realignment and true heart work will always have something to do with horses, but in the meantime, I needed to put the wheels in motion. I had been a little tentative with jumping back in as the loss of my soul horse Romeo in 2016 had taken a toll on my heart.

Mental/Mindset Reset

Go, Go, Go to No, No, No!

I had always been a rusher. I walk fast, eat fast, drink fast...is someone chasing me? No. So I am not sure where it comes from. But what I DO know is that when you rush through life, you cause your anxiety. Here is a quote about it that I love. Thank you to the wise person who shared this:

"Once she stopped rushing through life, she was amazed at how much more life she had time for".

When we live in a constant state of being and doing, it is exhausting. How can we ever possibly learn to relax when we always feel like we must be doing? That was me. So here I was in April 2020, the world was paralyzed and all the doing to be done did not exist. So, I figured it would be a great time to learn to embrace the energy of slowing down.

It is not easy to go from a lifetime of rushing through life to living each moment, but I had nothing but time to figure it all out. I would catch myself trying to create busywork, and I would stop myself and breathe and give myself permission to just be. When you are in this place and intentionally slow everything down, you begin to notice little things around you.

As a corporate escapee (after over 25 years), I lived in my head a lot and was very left-brained. I did not have much practice coming from a heart space until I learned how to do that from the horses, once I reconnected with them. I tried meditating and that was so difficult for me as I do not like to just sit anywhere and BE QUIET!! Me? Be quiet for that many minutes in a row? Yikes! Just like when I started yoga, I knew they'd kick me out...but they never did...I just kept my voice down. So, anyway, I learned that there are other ways to meditate that do not involve sitting for 30 minutes and trying to be quiet as that would never fly for me. I chose my morning walks as my walking meditation. Once I focused on my breathing and tuning in during my walks, I added my gratitudes and my daily intention. This is when the magic began to happen.

Flexibility is key, when you are tuned in and focusing on what you wish to bring into your life, you may be presented with options. The Universe is always working and will help you get into alignment if you are not. Sometimes you may have an opportunity that was not even on your radar and it may take you away from a path you thought you were supposed to take. Explore your options!

Master Manifestor

I began looking for furnished houses and nothing was cheap as it was still high season in Arizona. I knew that living in an apartment was not for me since I had been spoiled with living on acreage or large lots. I found a lovely, renovated home in an over 55 retirement area (yes, I felt young!) and thought that would be the perfect place to start over as it would force me to slow down and focus on what changes I needed to make for myself to find my happy. I moved in and was anticipating being there during the "off-season" April – October.

However, I recognized my energy had never felt settled since I had moved away from the area eight years earlier. So, since I was now learning the power of intention and gratitude and I was realizing how my life was transforming, I put it out there that I wanted to find an affordable place in a specific area, surrounded by horses and land. One of my other goals was to reduce expenses. I decided to do a search for a guest house in Cave Creek and see what may come up that I could consider in a few months when I was ready to move.

The reality about the power of manifesting and working with the Universe to help with your alignment is that you may need to jump on an opportunity and let go of whatever timetable YOU may THINK you have. A perfect place appeared. It was a house sitting/dog sitting opportunity located only a couple of blocks from where I used to live when I was married with horses at home.

Within two weeks I had met the homeowners, now new friends that were like family, and moved in to care for their dogs and beautiful home for at least a year while they were out of the country. The pandemic and subsequent vaccination rollout will dictate their return to the States. So, my daily gratitudes include the opportunity to live in this perfect physical space for me and my little Shihtty-Poo dog, Lucy, and our new extended family, two Clumber Spaniels.

This physical space also positioned me right in the middle of the horses I had longed to reconnect with. I was able to focus again on taking opportunities to help equine businesses create more sustainability and found a place to offer the concepts from this book in partnership with the horses.

After the loss of my soul horse Romeo in 2016, I had struggled to find MY place with the horses to do the work I know I am here to do. Horses are so much more than just a big, beautiful animal. For me, and many other young girls and boys who were lucky enough to experience horses at an early age, we understand. However, so many people are unaware of the life-changing lessons we can learn through connecting with them. When you truly allow yourself to tune in to your truth you can make such huge strides in creating more success in your life and even business.

By this time, I'd already lost and kept off 20 pounds, and my ability to truly manifest EXACTLY what I was seeking for my physical space back near the horses led my friends to begin to call me the "Master Manifestor," and it continues as I continue my daily practice of gratitude and setting an intention each day.

Beautiful Romeo working his magic at an equine coaching event.

Lessons Learned from the Horses

The importance of presence – Horses are prey animals so they are keenly aware of their surroundings at all times...just in case there is a big ole lion or bear, (or plastic bag) out there that could harm them. Many people think that dogs and horses are the same, but they are vastly different, as dogs are predators. Horses represent the epitome of presence which comes from their innate survival instinct. Their ability to "just be" in the present moment makes them such amazing examples for people to acknowledge and embrace. I remember when I was first learning how to engage with horses in this way how uncomfortable it was for me to just be. I think it's a tough one for many people and I'm still a work in progress, but I've learned how to permit myself to "just be."

For the most part, horses could care less about the past or future, unless of course they have been abused, they are focused on the here and now. When we adopt this way of living, we let go of so much of the story of our past or the "what ifs" of the future, and we can lessen the anxiety that comes with those fear-based behaviors. Take a breath, then another and just "be"...it feels good. So, when you get in a spin, remember the horses, and imagine a beautiful green pasture, take a breath and get present. This works!

Let's Get To IT!

My Self-Care BUCK UP!

What You are not Changing,
You are Choosing

Be Honest – *What's Not Working?*

I did not feel comfortable in my clothes nor did I like how I looked in the mirror. I would find myself being a little negative and just not happy with any aspect of my life. Authenticity is big for me, and I found that I was not living MY authentic life. How could I stress the importance of self-care and a positive mindset to others when I was toting around excess baggage myself? Nope...wasn't working!

Unapologetically You – *This is YOUR life, don't compare your journey to anyone else. What needs to change to help YOU create a more fulfilled life? Why is it important that you make this change?*

Self-care is the foundation of happiness and that is where my journey needed to start. I wanted to do this for ME, no one else. I wanted to release at least 20 pounds, commit to movement every day, and look and feel better in my clothes. As I learned...finally at age 55...it is more about what you are eating and drinking, along with movement that will bring about the results. Once I focused on that, without feeling deprived at all, the momentum built and the weight kept coming off.

Mindset/Perspective – Mentally, I wanted to release any negativity or energy that wasn't in alignment with where I wanted to be. You cannot have an optimistic mindset when you surround yourself with negativity. I was already pretty good at this but had a little more work to do.

Being a healthy and happy woman for ME is my intention and so I have adopted a lifestyle that supports the maintenance of that happy place!

Claim Desired Outcome – *Imagine how you will feel once you have embraced the positive changes. How will this affect your life?*

Once the weight started coming off and I had more energy I naturally was in a better mood. Every day I would wake up with a sense of excitement. I was proud of myself and celebrated my small successes like getting into that pair of jeans I'd held on to for so many years. Yes...you know you have a pair!

Kick It Into Gear – *Develop an action plan and get busy!*

I created an action plan for each of the three areas in my life of what I wanted to change or manifest. Then I drilled down into the details of what I needed to do to achieve the results I was seeking. Writing down your goals will help you with your accountability as well. (Don't worry, I created a form you can access later.)

Unbridle Your Passion – *Get excited about the new life you are creating!*

Experiencing success with releasing this weight was empowering. My clothes felt better, each day I was waking up extra early with this sense of excitement about what the day would bring. My energy shifted and people that I had known professionally were starting to come out of the woodwork and asking what I was doing. I realized after the suggestion from several friends that I should write a book about this positive journey, and here you are reading it!

Put Yourself in the Arena – *You have done the work and now it's time to confidently step through the gate!*

I wrote this book so I could help others take the reins and follow the steps that helped me create a new and fulfilling life! Nothing like documenting your journey to step into the arena!

Self-Care BUCK UP!

What You Are Not Changing,
You Are Choosing

Be Honest – *What's Not Working?*

_____

_____

_____

_____

Unapologetically You – *This is YOUR life; don't compare your journey to anyone else. What needs to change to help YOU create a more fulfilled life? Why is it important that you make this change?*

_____

_____

_____

_____

Claim Desired Outcome – *Imagine how you will feel once you have embraced the positive changes. How will this affect your life?*

_____

_____

_____

_____

Kick It Into Gear – *Develop an action plan and get busy.*

_____

_____

_____

_____

Unbridle Your Passion – *Get excited about the new life you are creating!*

_____

_____

_____

_____

Put Yourself in the Arena – *You've done the work and now it's time to confidently step through the gate!*

_____

_____

_____

_____

REASSESS (What's not working?)

Where are you today, at this moment? What is working and what is not? Are you satisfied or do you know there are more opportunities for happiness and potential, you just have not tapped into yet?

REALIGN (What will work and how do I get there?)

What is your passion? What lights you up? For businesses, are you still on track with your "Why" or have you derailed?

REIGNITE (How will I make it work?)

Imagine how you will feel once you have made your desired changes.

What is the ONE thing I will commit to change this week to bring me closer to my commitment to prioritizing my Self-Care?

My Self-Care Intention: I am committed to

_____

_____

_____

which will result in my dedication to prioritizing my self-care!

How will you hold yourself accountable for making changes and investing in yourself?

1.

2.

3.

SELF-CARE BONUS TIPS

The Difference between a "Routine" and a "Practice"

A "Practice" is something you do to reach a bigger goal. For example, meditation practice helps you gain more mindfulness; a yoga practice helps with centering and balance, etc. However, a "Routine" is usually done at a specific time and can get disrupted and hijacked as life gets in the way. If you live and die by your routine, what happens when it gets disrupted? Your whole life can get hijacked. So, as you'll see, I use the word "practice." This means that even though your intention was to get that walk, run or hike in first thing and then up pops a Zoom call you forgot about, no worries. Just get back on track when you can by taking a walk if you can't make it to a workout class. Make a practice of doing something in line with your overall goal of daily movement.

Here are a few FREE or low-cost ways to treat yourself to some self-care:
- Epsom salts in bath water and a couple of candles. Add some essential oil.
- Music is healing; create a playlist of your favorite songs. I have one for Country, and

one for Favorites, which is a compilation of everything from George Strait to Earth, Wind & Fire, etc. Choose the songs that make you happy and want to move! I listen to music daily and at this point rarely even turn on the TV.

- Adult coloring books, or children's coloring books for that matter! Pull out some bright colored pencils or pens and get lost in some pages. As a bonus, grab one that has inspirational sayings or whatever attracts you.
- Go for a walk or hike. Even 15 minutes can reset your mind and body.
- Breathe. There is so much benefit to focus on breath work as it is a total reset to being calmer. Here is an example of the power of breath and how our energy affects the horses.

I was doing a joint presentation with a friend and her miniature horses for a group of about 50 people in a networking group (back in the good old days when we could gather like that). Being very aware of energy and observing Bert, the mini horse, being very nervous I thought it would be a great exercise for the group to experience how within a few minutes you can take yourself into a calmer state and they would physically see the result with the horse.

I asked the group to take their seats and acknowledged the high energy in the room. It was a breakfast networking meeting, so everyone was busy in their minds with their next appointment, chugging coffee, or trying to connect with people in the room. I informed the group that horses are extremely sensitive to our energy and that the collective energy in the room was clearly being represented by the behavior of poor Bert. I asked them to observe how he was walking in circles and obviously not in a relaxed, comfortable state.

Then, I asked the group to help him out by first calming ourselves down with some breathing. One of my favorite breathing exercises that I use when I'm feeling anxious or can't get back to sleep is to inhale for the count of 5, hold for 5, exhale for 5 and hold for 5.

We repeated this breathing pattern three times, and the energy in the room was almost immediately calmer. Everyone witnessed the impact it had on Bert as he began to calm down and then lick and chew (which is one of the signs of a calmer state for horses).

People were amazed not only at the visible difference in Bert, but how different they felt. I suggested that this is a great exercise to do any time you feel yourself getting a little anxious, rushed, or stressed.

I use this breathing exercise frequently. You

know when you wake up in the middle of the night and your mind gives you a long to-do list? I've found that this breathing sequence helps me fall back to sleep easily.

MY NOTES – SELF-CARE

Relationships

"Be who you are and say what you feel because those who mind don't matter and those who matter don't mind." ~ Dr. Seuss

I felt that I had let myself go, and I had gone somewhere I did not want to be nor remain. I realized that it was not fair for me or my significant other at the time to continue the relationship. We were just going through the motions and I needed the space to figure out why I felt so out of place both in this relationship and the physical space in general.

With new beginnings, of course, comes endings and in my case, it was the end of an 8-year relationship with a great man, whom I will always be grateful for. It was time to move on for me to allow us both to find our own happiness. I was changing and knew in my heart that I needed to get back on track and in alignment with my calling to help others with the horses.

The last time I had decided to leave a long-term relationship was in 2006 when I chose to divorce my husband after 11 years. I remember I was upstairs in my home office in a beautiful big house in the Midwest on 13 acres with my custom dream barn in the back with 5 horses and big green pastures, but something was missing. "L.O.V.E." I had Oprah on the TV downstairs and instead of just background noise, for some reason, I tuned in.

The topic was *"women who stay in unhealthy relationships."* That perked my ears up, so I went downstairs to watch. Many of the women were enduring physical or emotional abuse and had no confidence so they felt trapped. I possessed self-confidence at a pretty early age due to the necessity to figure out self-sufficiency and by overcoming several major challenges, facing them head-on. I did not feel like I had no options like these women on TV. I realized that I was unhappy and staying in the marriage for all the wrong reasons.

I had a comfortable life with all the external appearances of success and happiness. I had a great casita in Scottsdale where I stayed when I commuted monthly for work, so a place to move to was not a problem. I realized that money and lifestyle are not everything and enduring verbal abuse was not working for me, so I ended it. I moved back full time to the casita in Scottsdale with three of my show horses and three dogs in tow and for the first time in a long time, I felt an inner strength return.

I guess this was my first introduction to how I had incorporated *Reassess, Realign, Reignite* to get my life back on track with my relationships.

Relationship with Self

The first step in achieving success in any kind of relationship is having a loving relationship with yourself. Yeah, I know, we have all heard it before, but everything truly starts and ends with you. If you do not appreciate, trust, respect, and love yourself, how do you expect another person to? How do you speak to yourself? Would you allow anyone to speak with your best friend the way you talk to yourself at times? Give yourself a Flippin break!

This is not easy as many of us have been conditioned by society and in some cases toxic relationships to dwell on our imperfections if they don't meet the "socially acceptable" standards. Well, I am here to tell you that the sooner you stop listening to the judgmental noise, the more at peace you will become. We are all individuals with perfectly imperfect parts of ourselves that make us unique!

The insecure ones that do not like to be unique are the ones that try to become someone they have been told is the image of beauty. I think beauty comes from the inside and your ability to embrace your imperfections and uniqueness. I have a fang and that is all I see when I smile in a picture (now you will focus on it too!), but that is what makes me unique and far from perfect. Perfection is overrated.

Self-talk

'Thoughts become Things" as Mike Dooley from, *The Universe Talks*, tells us. And it is so true. Words are so powerful! Once you truly realize that you can create your reality simply by the words you are using, you will begin to be more mindful. So many people disrespect themselves by constantly degrading themselves or focusing on their flaws or faults. We would not let anyone else talk to us the way that we sometimes speak to ourselves. I challenge you to think about that.

Why do we tend to go to the negative when something happens and commonly blame ourselves? Most likely it has nothing to do with us, but we take on ownership and unnecessary self-doubt. When you are in a funk, it is important to remember that the longer you stay there, thinking funkish thoughts, the longer you will remain there, and you are blocking your possibilities. It is up to YOU to take a breath and start focusing on your positive attributes and successes.

Believe in yourself and get excited about your ability to create the life you desire! Understand how powerful you are and stand in your authenticity. Stop living for others and being concerned about what they think.

Recovering Perfectionist

I have always been my biggest critic and continue to hold myself to a high bar. Throughout my days as an employee, this was great if you are a high achiever and make your bosses look good. However, it can also create impatience with others who do not hold that same trait.

As an entrepreneur, holding yourself to a higher standard is almost a necessity alongside tenacity, perseverance, and resilience! However, you must learn patience as collaborations are important. I'm still a work in progress with this one, but once we allow ourselves to be human, not superhuman, and make the mistakes and learn from them, we really can embrace what a gift that is. Perceived mistakes can lead you down wonderful and unexpected paths that expose you to life-changing insights

Some of my perfectionist tendencies may have come from the years of showing horses. I was an equitation rider, which meant, every last detail had to be perfect. This was something I began at age 12 and is probably where some of my confidence comes from. When you are showing a horse, you are essentially on stage.

The Missouri State Fair coliseum was my first big stage, then progressed to The American Royal in Kansas City. Once I reconnected with horses many years later, I traveled across the nation for big shows with my Paints and Quarter Horses. That stage was the one place I felt appreciated. With that also comes a lot of judgment about how you look, from your outrageously priced outfits for some classes and overall picture with the horse. When you are showing at a National and World Class level like I was, you put a lot of pressure on yourself for that picture of perfection.

Added to that was my ex-husband who was very competitive and put additional pressure on me to win as we were spending a significant amount of money. I was fortunate to have some amazing horses I partnered with which contributed to some titles, and successes, however, that added pressure can result in self-doubt and you get in your head. This is not a good place to be when working with horses as they are so tuned in to you that you can sabotage yourself and a world championship ride if you are not being present. Been there, done that before I knew this little secret about how to connect with the horses.

Apply this to normal living. Think about a time when you were so focused on perfection that you almost became obsessed with it. When we are in this headspace, we do not think about if this end goal is in our best interest or if it may be our Ego speaking to us. Ask yourself if your desire for this accomplishment is coming from an ego space or a heart space. When we come from a heart space it will feel right and things may fall into place easier. Whereas, when we are coming from Ego, we get more judgmental of ourselves and others and it feels difficult. I'm all about the feels.

The constant striving for perfection can also deplete you as nothing is ever good enough. It's as if you are in competition with yourself. Learn to let it go and do your best. Your best is perfect.

Learning to Love Myself

Life is a journey and how we embrace or resist each lesson will lay the foundation for our success and sense of fulfillment in our personal and business lives. Most of us have experienced a life event that impacted the way we chose to proceed on our journey through the various chapters of our lives. In some cases, we have made choices for self-protection and in other cases, we did not know we had a choice.

We do the best we can with what we know at that moment and in many cases, although we think we are protecting ourselves, we are building a wall against that which we need to face in order to heal. How we feel about ourselves on the inside affects everything on the outside. When you see yourself as more you will attract and retain more overall success and fulfillment.

I'm going to share a little history about my relationships not to play a victim, as I never chose that path, but to share my journey which may resonate with some of you and possibly open up a door for your own healing to begin.

I endured several years of sexual abuse by a family member and family friend when I was young. Then my father left my mother one month after their 25th wedding celebration when I was 16. This divorce necessitated the sale of my horse, Dooby, who was my world. I am much younger than most of my siblings and due to my choice of spending so many summers and time away from home with the horses, I did not have a really close relationship with most of them. This caused me to feel that it was up to me alone to take care of myself at the ripe age of about 16, and therefore constructed the first of a few walls.

Protective Wall Number 1 =Abandonment
Both parents moved away from my hometown of Lawrence, Kansas after the divorce, and I chose to remain with my friends to finish high school. So, in my young teenage mind, I felt that I needed to become self-sufficient and never rely on anyone

else. I am from a big family but being the youngest of six, everyone had already moved away except for one sister who did not want me to live with her.

Wall number 1 impacted my ability to trust men or let them get close for fear that they would leave me. The sexual abuse kind of played into this as well. I would date for a few months, and then if I felt they were getting too serious I would break it off. In my twisted head, I thought better I end it before someone hurts me...yeah...pretty jacked up, and if any of you men I hurt are reading this, I'm truly sorry!

Since I never really processed or got any help with the abandonment issues and sexual trauma from my childhood that did not help me so much with my relationships.

The thing is, I had not done ANY of my own work around some of the deep-seated issues, as I had the walls up, so I was making the same mistakes. I was trying to find my happy IN a relationship. NO. I am sure you have read it before, but YOU must do the work, and find your happy and work through some issues with a professional or on your own, but it is a journey you need to take. At this point in my life, I am really happy to say that I've finally learned this lesson...yay me! I'm still working on ME for ME, so whenever the Universe delivers my Prince Charming, I'll allow myself to show up and be a great partner.

Protective Wall Number 2 = Heartbreak

Due to the pain of losing my horse in 1980, I slammed the door on anything to do with horses. Boxed up my walls lined with ribbons, trophies, and Breyer horse models, never to be opened again. I built a wall to protect myself from that loss I felt from having to say goodbye to the one thing that meant the most in the world to me. The horses.

It was not until 1996 when I allowed myself to admire a picture of a colleague's horse on her desk at work that I began to break this wall down and let horses back into my life. One of the best decisions I'd made, and it taught me the especially important lesson about reconnecting with a passion that was still living in my heart. In addition, as an adult, I chose to explore the connection I felt and learn more about horses. This newfound wisdom and appreciation for the profound lessons they can teach us, helped me to pursue a path to educate others about the amazing healing abilities of horses. Goodbye protective wall, hello reignited passion and purpose!

Relationship with Others

"People come into your life for a Reason, a Season or a Lifetime..." ~ *Unknown*

We will live through several chapters in our lifetime. With each chapter, most of us are learning life lessons and experiences. As we progress through life, we either learn the lessons, seek our own self and/or professional development, or choose the path of staying the same. That path of stagnation was never an option for me, by choice. We will meet people throughout these different chapters and as I've come to realize they all have such an important role.

The people you met during your childhood and into your high school days knew a completely different version of you than those you met as you entered your adult life. Those you knew as colleagues throughout your corporate life, knew a different person than you may be post-corporate life and into your entrepreneurial journey such as I've taken.

Every person has an individual journey and personality as it would be dreadfully boring if we were all the same! How we interact with others is so important as in addition to personalities we all have the beliefs that ring true for us. In most cases, you will resonate with individuals who are most closely aligned with your value system and feel a sense of hesitation around those with different beliefs. How we learn acceptance and how to embrace our differences can lead to creating a more positive outcome for everyone.

For so long I was concerned about what people thought of me. I wanted them to like me. I didn't want anyone to be upset with me. Do you know how exhausting that is? What also happens is that you aren't always true to yourself when trying to please others. This leads back to the authenticity that I've mentioned several times. Some people are going to love you and others will not like you at all for whatever reason. Don't spend any energy on it. I sure wish I'd learned that lesson many years ago!

Very few people have a *Leave it to Beaver* family upbringing and so we walk through the life experiences, both good and bad, that our parents have endured. We can either choose to break or continue the cycle. We can also choose to be a victim or not. If you have children you may want to consider this. I chose not to have children, so I am in NO WAY an expert, however, we all have a choice to break a cycle if it's unhealthy.

We cannot choose our families; however, we can choose how we manage our relationships with them. Of course, there will always be challenges and family dynamics, however, if you are always the one trying to make the effort for a relationship, pay attention. For those with dysfunction junction families, the sooner you learn that you do have a choice whether or not to participate in the drama, the more empowered you will feel.

As I have mentioned in several parts of this book, who you surround yourself with is so important. Does your circle feed on negativity and take joy in judging others? We do take on the energy of those around us so "Who's in Your First-Class Cabin"? Who have you invited into your close circle? Choose wisely. In some instances, there may be no family on the plane, and that is OK. We can create our "family" with friends.

Relationship with Money

Since I started working at an early age due to the necessity to ensure I had the income to pay my living expenses, I have always had an interesting relationship with money. When I began my corporate career at the ripe old age of 18 and started making what I thought was great money, compared to my Dillon's Grocery Store cashier days in High School, I fell into the dangerous credit card doom loop. As I continued to progress through corporate and make more money, I spent a little more too. I got into a REALLY bad habit of buying brand spankin new cars every year, and just rolling the debt from car payment to car payment. You see I did not have any financial guidance as I was on my own and felt I just needed to figure it out. And, that habit lasted into my marriage.

I was married to a man who was raised in the country club lifestyle and very flashy so we had to keep up the appearances of all that material bullshit. The reality being that we were in debt for all that outward appearance. In 1998, I also began showing horses again, so a big chunk of my corporate paycheck went to my CRAZY expensive habit of showing my horses around the country. A couple of my horses cost the same or more than most people's luxury cars. But I was having fun, had great credit, and did not think about the fact that just because I was making great money, that did not mean my expenses should almost match my monthly income!

As I have mentioned, I chose to accept a layoff, leave the corporate world, and start Unbridle It, LLC. After a couple of months when the severance depleted, reality started to sink in. I did not want to go back to a corporate job, I wanted to help people and make a difference with the horses. I also had three horses to support which was about a $3000/mo. expense as well as an expensive car payment. It all came crashing down a few years later when I had to face the reality that I needed to claim bankruptcy. Nothing I am proud of, but my poor decisions with a lack of support had led me down this path. Again, no blame, I claim it and have since got myself out of the mess and back to a strong credit rating.

So, I have experienced both spectrums of living a very comfortable life, and then freaking the shit out about how to pay my bills. I sold one of my horses which helped pay for my divorce and some bills before the bankruptcy. With no one to ask for advice, I made another poor decision of dipping into my growing retirement accounts. Yep, another bad decision, but in my mid-40s I did not think about the longer-term repercussions of that one.

I found that even when I was making great money, I was coming from a place of lack or fear that it would run out. When we are always putting that fear energy towards our interactions with money, how could it possibly result in a positive outcome for income?

It wasn't until I started appreciating what I had and changing my energy and words around money that things changed. More money would come in. I was no longer blocking it with the energy of lack. So, some of you may be thinking that this sounds a bit Pollyanna-ish, but no. I adopted this way of thinking after losing a couple of clients, moving out on my own at the onset of the pandemic, and realizing something had to change. I was also intentional with reducing expenses.

There is so much power in your mindset and intention and especially around money. What you focus on grows, so are you focusing on lack or abundance? Where your focus goes, energy flows. Don't focus on what you don't want!

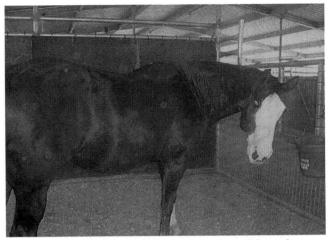
I love this picture of Sassy surrounded by orbs.

Lessons Learned from the Horses

The importance of authenticity – Show up! Embrace who you are, not who you think you are supposed to be. You are here on your journey and that journey is not a competition with others.

As I've mentioned horses tune in to your truth. If you show up with a big smile and saying "I love horses!" however, your insides are in a knot from childhood experience with being bucked off or bitten and you are honestly afraid, the horse will sense your fear. However, if you claim your fear instead of hiding from it, the horse will be more willing to engage as you are being honest with your feelings.

Most people are not nearly as sensitive to energy as horses, however, when you show up for life more authentically, people will respond more positively. This results in more successful relationships both personally and professionally.

The Original Unbridle It Team

Let's Get To IT!

My Relationship BUCK UP!

*What You Are Not Changing,
You Are Choosing*

Be Honest – *What's Not Working?*
I was not happy with my relationship with my significant other nor my environment. I found myself at times reverting to a lack mindset which was not healthy.

Unapologetically You – *This is YOUR life, don't compare your journey to anyone else. What needs to change to help YOU create a more fulfilled life? Why is it important that you make this change?*
I needed to remove myself physically, emotionally, and mentally from the situation and reconnect with myself to figure out how to create my happy. My life wasn't working for me, and I didn't like how I was feeling in my relationships.

Claim Desired Outcome – *Imagine how you will feel once you have embraced the positive changes. How will this affect your life?*
Once I take responsibility for my own life again,

I can choose to create my destiny.

Kick It Into Gear – *Develop an action plan and get busy!*

My action plan started with the decision to leave the relationship with a great man and move out on my own. I took the time to do the work on self-love and learning what I needed for myself, no one else.

Unbridle Your Passion – *Get excited about the new life you are creating!*

The physical space and independence lead to opportunities to tune in and experience the positive changes that my decisions and new intentions were manifesting.

Put Yourself in the Arena – *You have done the work and now it's time to confidently step through the gate!*

Once I made the physical move, I stepped into my new life and mantra. ***Be You, Do You, For You***

Relationship BUCK UP!

What You Are Not Changing,
You Are Choosing

Be Honest – *What's Not Working?*

_____

_____

_____

_____

Unapologetically You – *This is YOUR life; don't compare your journey to anyone else. What needs to change to help YOU create a more fulfilled life? Why is it important that you make this change?*

_____

_____

_____

_____

Claim Desired Outcome – *Imagine how you will feel once you have embraced the positive changes. How will this affect your life?*

_____

_____

_____

_____

Kick It Into Gear – *Develop an action plan and get busy.*

_____

_____

_____

_____

Unbridle Your Passion – *Get excited about the new life you are creating!*

_____

_____

_____

_____

Put Yourself in the Arena – *You've done the work and now it's time to confidently step through the gate!*

_____

_____

_____

_____

REASSESS (What's not working?)

Where are you today, at this moment? What is working and what is not? Are you satisfied or do you know there are more opportunities for happiness and potential, you just have not tapped into yet?

REALIGN (What will work and how do I get there?)

What is your passion? What lights you up? For businesses, are you still on track with your "Why" or have you derailed?

REIGNITE (How will I make it work?)

Imagine how you will feel once you have made your desired changes.

What is the ONE thing I will commit to change this week that will bring me closer to my commitment to prioritizing my Relationships?

My Relationship Intention: I am committed to

_____

_____

_____

_____

which will result in my dedication to prioritizing my relationships.

How will you hold yourself accountable for making changes and investing in yourself?

1.

2.

3.

MY NOTES – RELATIONSHIPS

Alignment with Your Purpose

"Don't ask what the world needs. Ask what makes you come alive and go do it. Because what the world needs is people who have come alive." ~ Howard Thurman

I know that my true desire and purpose is to help people understand how horses are natural healers and loving partners. With my business experience and passion on the subject, I also knew that my value was to truly help the equine business owners or "Equinepreneurs" as I call them. Many of the people who work with horses are passionate about their work but do not have the business and marketing background necessary to get their businesses off the ground.

This is where I knew I could be of assistance, coupled with the fact that I understand how the horses can change lives. One of the challenges with many amazing practitioners in this population is that their businesses are not sustainable, and they cannot afford the assistance necessary to market themselves to begin to create positive income flow.

One of the first things I did was to create a Facebook Group (Unbridled Equinepreneurs). Realizing that mental health is one of the biggest challenges in the country, and the reality that it was about to become even worse with the quarantine isolation, I saw (and still do) a real opportunity for those businesses who offer healing with the horses to step up and make a huge difference.

I would like to clear up one misconception that so many people have. Not all work like this with horses is "therapy" albeit it truly IS therapeutic. If you need the assistance of a licensed therapist, please ensure you seek a true equine therapy practitioner. However, working with an experienced equine coach can many times help you move past your roadblocks and onto greener pastures...so to speak! I am happy to help you determine which may be the best fit for your particular situation.

Since I had begun my daily gratitude practice and setting intentions, various opportunities were coming to me from several areas. One of my daily gratitudes is, "I'm grateful for the money and opportunity that comes easily to me." Even though I was focused on what I THOUGHT I needed to do with my Equinepreneurs, the Universe was giving me what I was asking for, and I realized it.

So, when a newly reconnected acquaintance asked me if I was interested in an opportunity to help with marketing for one of her clients, at first, I hesitated, as again, I thought I was supposed to work the horse people. But the reality was, I needed a stable income in the meantime. I am so grateful for the opportunity this client provided as it offered a great service for the community. It also helped me reduce my credit card debt and live a little without watching every penny. After the project, I was able to focus on completing this book, as well as, on my game plan for helping Equinepreneurs.

Pay Attention!

When you begin to gain clarity on what you genuinely want in your life or business, people who are in your same energetic lane of traffic will suddenly appear in your life to help you on this path. Do not be so focused on what you THINK you are supposed to do and miss out on opportunities that may take you on a different adventure but still support your main goal.

When you put your desires out there, be prepared to act on them when they appear! You can always return to your original path if that is what is calling to you, or you may discover the detour leads to even more fulfillment.

This journey is yours, so every choice offers a

learning opportunity.

You may experience a lot of judgment from others when exploring what is most in alignment with who you are and what kind of impact you would like to make. It takes a lot of resilience to keep on going and turn off the noise. The path may not be a cakewalk, but the lessons you experience along the way make the journey worth it once you have arrived.

Spiritual

The power of gratitude and intention and tuning in to my intuitive wisdom is what set this year apart for me. Sure, I had read the *Law of Attraction* and tried to be mindful of my words and understood the power of words, but I was not embracing this practice consistently. That was, until I chose once again to change all aspects of my life at age 55 and decided I had better be pretty intentional as the world was entering a place of total chaos. The ability to tune in to your intuition for guidance is something we all have, but it requires some work and practice.

For most of my life, I associated Spirituality with Religion as I did not understand the difference. It wasn't until I was in my 40s, when I became more in tune with my intuitive abilities and energy, that I understood that there is such a difference between the two. I was intrigued and wanted to learn more. I had always been keenly interested in astrology, crystals, and the supernatural. I was introduced to numerology and that provided so much clarification, guidance, and confirmation of what I intuitively felt about me and my life. Two women who introduced me to the power of numerology are Elizabeth Summers and Karen Winkelman, and I'd highly recommend both of them. I've included their websites at the end of the book.

Shortly before I graduated high school, I had reconnected with my father and we arranged for me to move out to California with him and his girlfriend. During the trip, out of the blue, my dad told me something I have never forgotten. "Leeanne, you have a gift. I see it in you, and I had the same gift, but I let it go and did not work on it. Don't lose it, you are powerful." I asked him to explain and he would not go into it.

I kind of just let it go for many years until my interest in astrology and energetic connection became stronger. During astrology and shamanic readings, something would always come up about my intuitive abilities and that I am a "wise woman." That would remind me of that conversation with my father. I did not embrace what they were saying until many years later once I was no longer in the left-brained corporate life and had some time to explore a little deeper. I also learned that my paternal grandmother had an intuitive gift yet was institutionalized for it as it wasn't accepted back in her time. She and I always had a special connection, and now I understood why, unfortunately after she has passed on.

Today, energy work, astrology, numerology, and other semi woo-woo stuff is a part of who I am. I love working with the energy of the moon and experiencing how powerful it is for setting intentions and manifesting what you genuinely want to welcome in or release from your life.

I was raised by a very Catholic mother and an Atheist father. The agreement was that we had to go to church until we were about 13. So, my childhood bestie Nancy and I would go, pick up a bulletin and sit up in the balcony and then get the giggles as we would spot something funny, like an older woman's blue hair. I did not know what it was, but there was something I just had a resistance to at an early age about the church.

It was not until I was a little older and understood some of the hypocrisy that came into play that I understood why I felt as I did. How could people be so judgmental about others and do things during the week and think that going to church on Sunday would wipe the slate clean? It never felt right so as soon as I aged out of the family restriction I only went to mass when it was required.

Lessons Learned from the Horses

Horses are highly sensitive and empathic, which is one of the reasons they are so amazing in helping to cut through to the truth of a situation. Horses will call bullshit if you are not being honest. One of the most profound experiences I had, and continue to use with the horses, is to help people walk in their truth.

Susan F. Moody and I hosted a *Create Your Own Success Story* retreat with horses which followed some of the concepts in her book, *Cz The Day!* Part of the exercise was for each participant to speak aloud their intention. The women would state their phrases about what they wished to create and I would pay attention to how the horses responded. If the woman spoke confidently about what she had written, the horse would continue effortlessly through the labyrinth.

However, if the woman was a bit more tentative or didn't believe the words she had written, the horse would stop. This opened up the opportunity to explore just what it was about those words that she wasn't believing herself so we could work on that. Once we broke through, she could restate her intention and we knew she was speaking her truth when the horse continued on the path with her.

Let's Get To IT!

My Alignment with Purpose
BUCK UP!

What You Are Not Changing,
You Are Choosing

Be Honest – *What's Not Working?*

I felt completely out of alignment with my passion for working with horses to make a difference. How could I encourage people to pursue their passion with a positive outlook when I wasn't living that truth?

Unapologetically You – *This is YOUR life, don't compare your journey to anyone else. What needs to change to help YOU create a more fulfilled life? Why is it important that you make this change?*

I knew all change comes from within and we must get to the point where we will no longer just remain where we are. Change isn't easy for so many, but for me, once I make up my mind, I do a clean sweep of every aspect of my life. The importance for me was that I felt out of alignment and it was time for me to buck up and embrace my purpose of helping others on a larger scale.

I needed to return to a physical space that was more in alignment with where I wanted to live on my own with an ultimate goal of returning to Cave Creek in an area surrounded by horses.

Claim Desired Outcome – *Imagine how you will feel once you have embraced the positive changes. How will this affect your life?*

Once I decided to BUCK UP and create MY Happy, almost immediately I felt a sense of relief and excitement about creating something I WAS in alignment with. I did not have a clear plan at the time, but the first step was to make the decision that the life I was living wasn't working, something needed to change, and it was all up to me. Horses are my heart. Once I can reconnect and live in an area where I can be around them daily, I will be more grounded and fulfilled.

Kick It Into Gear – *Develop an action plan and get busy!*

Master Manifestor in action – the new house I moved into was surrounded by horse property. A beautiful horse ranch with an innovative horsemanship program was nearby. I intentionally reached out to see how I could become involved with what they were creating and they embraced the idea.

Unbridle Your Passion – *Get excited about the new life you are creating!*

Opportunities presented themselves for more involvement and creative ways to offer solutions with the horses for people seeking connection and an outlet during the continued pandemic and world drama.

Put Yourself in the Arena – *You have done the work and now it's time to confidently step through the gate!*

I am now creating collaborative programs highlighting the connection with the horses literally in the arena, my stage of choice!

Alignment with Purpose
BUCK UP!

What You Are Not Changing,
You Are Choosing

Be Honest – *What's Not Working?*

_____

_____

_____

_____

Unapologetically You – *This is YOUR life; don't compare your journey to anyone else. What needs to change to help YOU create a more fulfilled life? Why is it important that you make this change?*

_____

_____

_____

_____

Claim Desired Outcome – *Imagine how you will feel once you have embraced the positive changes. How will this affect your life?*

_____

_____

_____

_____

Kick It Into Gear – *Develop an action plan and get busy.*

_____

_____

_____

_____

Unbridle Your Passion – *Get excited about the new life you are creating!*

_____

_____

_____

_____

Put Yourself in the Arena – *You've done the work and now it's time to confidently step through the gate!*

_____

_____

_____

_____

REASSESS (What's not working?)

Where are you today, at this moment? What is working and what is not? Are you satisfied or do you know there are more opportunities for happiness and potential, you just have not tapped into yet?

REALIGN (What will work and how do I get there?)

What is your passion? What lights you up? For businesses, are you still on track with your "Why" or have you derailed?

REIGNITE (How will I make it work?)

Imagine how you will feel once you have made your desired changes.

What is the ONE thing I will commit to change this week that will bring me closer to my commitment to prioritizing my Alignment with Purpose?

My Alignment with Purpose Intention:
I am committed to

_____

_____

_____

_____

which will result in my dedication to prioritizing my alignment with purpose.

How will you hold yourself accountable for making changes and investing in yourself?

1.

2.

3.

MY NOTES – ALIGNMENT WITH YOUR PURPOSE

TIME TO DO
THE WORK

Buck Up Worksheets and Goal Planner

"Sometimes the strength within you is not a big fiery flame for everyone to see, it's just a spark that whispers so softly, "Keep going. You got this!" ~ Unknown

My 90 Day Result - Personal

I released 18 pounds the first 90 days. Notice I say "released," not lost, as I don't want to FIND it again...the power of words! I am down over 20 pounds now, nine months later, and have kept it off. I had relocated to a safe space with my dog that also allowed me to reduce expenses. Within 180 days I was back living in a rural horse-filled neighborhood, and had reconnected with the horses. In addition, I was allowing myself to have FUN and really tap into who I was at 55 and what I wanted.

I noticed that I was waking up almost every morning with a sense of excitement for the day!

This holds true today. Don't get me wrong, I can still get triggered by something, but instead of falling into a funk I easily catch myself, go through my steps, and pull myself out of it quickly.

My 90 Day Result - Professional

I saw the pandemic as a perfect opportunity for exhausted business owners, who are usually focused on building their businesses, to switch their focus to their foundation. What is working, what is not working, and fix it. I was offering marketing assessments and helping people get real to determine if they were aligned with their businesses.

I made changes to my existing client base; some were my decision and others were dictated by lack of funding. I decided to get back to my passion for helping Equinepreneurs (as I call them) with their equine inspired businesses as I saw such a huge need for the horse healing to come to the forefront. As I was showing my gratitude for opportunities, they kept appearing, seemingly out of nowhere, but it was all very intentional, as I came to realize. I was grateful for a lucrative opportunity that temporarily took me away from focusing on the Equinepreneurs, but it offered me a great source of income. When opportunities appear, you jump on them, and can get back on track. This was about the time I decided that I should write a book to document these amazing changes I was experiencing.

Daily List of Self-Care To-Dos

Before you get out of bed (and preferably before you grab your phone to see who liked your last FB post):

1) Breathe, take at least 3 deep breaths. My favorite is inhaling for 5 seconds, hold it for 5 seconds, exhale for 5 seconds, and hold the exhale for 5 seconds.

2) Stretch, slowly wake your body up with some gentle stretches instead of jumping out of bed like a wild person.

3) Say at least 3 things you are grateful for and set an intention for the day. If you are just working on the one intention for the week, that is fine, repeat it. Remember, stating your gratitudes and intentions have no power unless you a) truly believe it, b) are mindful with your words so you don't self-sabotage, c) you are taking action to bring them to life.

Words are immensely powerful so when you are stating your gratitudes say them as if they are already happening and when they start coming true, keep it up, as it is working!

Personal example: *I am grateful for my strong immune system and a healthy body.*

For Entrepreneurs, maybe something like: *I am grateful for the steady flow of income and clients.*

Worksheets and Goal Planner
BUCK UP!

What You Are Not Changing,
You Are Choosing

Be Honest – *What's Not Working?*

_____

_____

_____

_____

Unapologetically You – *This is YOUR life; embrace the life you desire. Don't compare to anyone else.*

_____

_____

_____

_____

Claim Desired Outcome – *How do you want to feel when you achieve? Why is it important that you make this change? How will this affect your life?*

_____

_____

_____

_____

Kick It Into Gear – *Develop an action plan and get busy*

_____

_____

_____

_____

Unbridle Your Passion – *What needs to change to help you create a more fulfilled life?*

_____

_____

_____

_____

Put Yourself in the Arena – *You've done the work and now it's time to confidently step through the gate!*

_____

_____

_____

_____

REASSESS (What's not working?)

Where are you today, at this moment? What is working and what is not? Are you satisfied or do you know there are more opportunities for happiness and potential, you just have not tapped into yet?

REALIGN (What will work and how do I get there?)

What is your passion? What lights you up? For businesses, are you still on track with your "Why" or have you derailed?

REIGNITE (How will I make it work?)

Imagine how you will feel once you have made your desired changes.

What is the ONE thing I will commit to change this week that will bring me closer toward my commitment to improving my _____ ***?***

My_____ Intention:

I am committed to

_____

_____

_____

_____

which will result in my dedication to prioritizing my _____.

How will you hold yourself accountable for making changes and investing in yourself?

1.

2.

3.

Below is a from the goal planner that I use. The one you can download on "The Book" page at www.unbridleit.com has 4 Goals with their Target Date and list of 5 Actions for each. For My Goal Planner, I used Goal #1 as Physical Environment, Goal #2 Well-being/Self-Care, Goal #3 Monday, and Goal #4 Relationships.

My Ultimate _____**Goal is:**

_____

_____

_____

_____

Example: **My Ultimate** Self-Care **Goal is:** Reduce twenty pounds, tone up, and improve my strength to feel better and look great in my clothes.

Goal: (specify area, ex: Reduce weight)

#1_____

Target Date: _____
(specify a date you wish to accomplish this goal)

Action Steps:

1) _____

2) _____

3) _____

4) _____

5) _____

This is just an example. I suggest setting several specific goals for each of your Ultimate Goals, each with specific action plans. Visit "The Book" tab at www.unbridleit.com to download a full-sized copy to use.

MY NOTES ON WORKSHEETS
AND GOAL PLANNER

BOSSMARE'S TIPS FROM THE TRAIL

Bossmare aka Lead mare

The horse that guides the herd to food and water, controls the daily routine and movement of the herd, and ensures the general well-being of the herd.

Unbridled Lessons

When you are working with a horse, regardless of if it is on the ground or riding, you cannot be up in your head. You must be present and intentional with your thoughts. Horses will feel your incongruency if you are not fully present and that disconnect can lead to miscommunication. Working with horses is a partnership and they are usually willing to dance with you when you are communicating clearly with no agenda.

Translate that one to your personal and professional relationships. If you are so busy trying to get your agenda across and not listening, you open yourself up to potentially getting bucked off...so to say. You may cause issues in a personal relationship or you may lose a business deal.

Horses are not judgmental, and they do not compare themselves to other horses. This alone is a great lesson for us two-leggeds to adopt! You do not see a herd of horses talking about how jealous they are of Trigger's beautiful head or making fun of Flicka for the braids her human put in her mane. They care about their safety every moment, period. They do not care what you look like, how much money you have, or what you drive. What they DO care about is that you are showing up authentically. As a prey animal, they are always keenly aware of their surroundings. When you work with a horse and are not being fully present or have your own agenda, they will be cautious and reluctant to engage with you. However, when you are fully present, they are much more willing participants.

Translate this one into leadership. The lead mare or "bossmare" is not the loudest most boisterous horse in the herd, she is the one that is most trusted as she is aware of how to keep the herd safe not a personal agenda.

When I started Unbridle It back in 2008, I created my title as "Bossmare" and I still use it for my email, Bossmare@Unbridleit.com. I guess now I'm the Buck Up Bossmare!

Don't Let the Universe Put You in a Time Out!

When you push yourself to the brink of exhaustion, the Universe will knock you on your ass. This has happened to me on more than one occasion, so I have learned that I'd better listen to the hints or deal with the consequences.

My first experience was when I was working

one of my corporate jobs with a lot of responsibility as an Account Executive for a hospitality technology company. I was loaded up with some very demanding clients and there was a change in leadership that was stressing most of us out. Also, I was traveling around the country showing my horses (which was fun, but still incredibly stressful at times when going for a National title).

I was sitting in my office when suddenly my peripheral vision started closing in and I felt strange. I saw squiggles and could not focus. I called out to the woman in the next office and told her my symptoms...but kept working...cause that's how I roll. I went to my doctor a few days later and he gave me a warning that if I didn't make some kind of change to reduce the stress in my life, I'd end up with a heart attack and I was only 35. Part of my stress was my unhappy marriage as well. So, I took a leave of absence to try to regain my health and made some changes, but not as I should have.

Fast forward to 2015. It was day eight of a 14-day trade show schedule and just as the International Housewares Show in Chicago is opening its doors, I am in the booth alone and start to feel weird. I had a memory from 15 years before, but this time was worse. I could not talk to tell the woman in the booth what was going on. I saw the squiggles again and my left arm was feeling numb. I picked up a tent card to try to read it, but no words would come out of my mouth and it seemed like there was no signal from my brain. Uh, yeah, this was different and scary.

So, being the responsible employee and strong woman that I was, I decided to just drink some water and it would pass. Not so much. When my boss came back to the tradeshow booth, I was able to convey to him that something was wrong, but the words still were not coming. He told me to go get checked out, so I went to the EMT station and they wanted to call an ambulance. I knew the hospital was close (and did not want to pay for an ambulance as I did not have insurance) so I got in a cab and headed to the ER.

The interesting thing with ERs is they take possible heart attacks very seriously and I got to go to the front of the line and headed up to the stroke unit. Oh, joy, here comes the IV...and why are you giving me a shot in my stomach? It was not so fun. I just remember them asking why I was there as I was a healthy woman, and I was like, uh y 'all are the doctors, you tell me! I always seem to have a way of making light of situations even when I was scared to death thinking that I may have had a stroke.

They wheeled a woman in the first night to be my roommate, that was an apparent drug addict based on the conversations that were easy to overhear through the curtain. Seems like she was a frequent guest at the hospital as the first responders and nursing staff knew her by name. However, they have to treat everyone with dignity and the same level of care based on symptoms. She liked to watch Jerry Springer and it just all seemed so fitting! The nurses kept coming in and apologizing as she was a loud one as she was detoxing. They finally moved her or discharged her.

My next roommate was an older woman who did not speak English and kept ripping her IVs out so the alarm would go off and wake me up...every 15 minutes. Again, I just took it in stride as they kept trying to figure out what had happened to me.

Morning of day three in the stroke unit of Chicago Mercy, this 13-year-old female Doogie Howser (ok I'm sure she was older, but still) comes in and again asks me "So why are you here?" and again, I ask her the same thing as I'm not getting paid to be the doctor. "Well, we think you may have had a TIA (transient ischemic attack), but we aren't seeing anything on the tests that confirm it, so we are diagnosing a "Complicated Migraine."

"Complicated" I guess since I always associated migraines with headaches, which I did not have. But then I remember back when I had the first episode that the neurologist told me then it was some kind of migraine. Once again, I got the lecture about managing stress, and this time I took it more to heart as I knew I did not want to end up back in the hospital being poked and prodded again!

A couple of years later I suffered from adrenal failure for pushing myself too hard for a new business that I was in, but I saw the signs and slowed my ass down before things got worse. These are just a couple of examples I went through because I did not heed the warnings that the Universe will send you when you are pushing yourself too hard.

Gratitude and Intention

Since about 2018 I had always talked about the power of gratitude and how tuning into your intuition for guidance was so powerful. I also have a circle of intuitive guides that I call in for support and assistance. Usually, it is just to confirm what I am already feeling, but it is nice to receive that reassurance.

One of the most important changes I made that powered my transformation was that I began becoming much more intentional about starting each day at a slower pace. Instead of jumping out of bed, chugging a cup of coffee while watching the news before racing out to walk my dog before a morning meeting, I...slowed...down. Before I even got out of bed, I did some stretching and started saying my gratitudes and an intention for the day.

I began drinking a cup of coffee and looking for meaningful posts or beautiful images of the sunrise or desert beauty that I could share on Facebook and Instagram instead of listening to the increasingly alarming news about this pandemic.

When I went for my walk, I noticed the beauty around me and started to truly think about what I wanted and focused on being grateful for everything I had. I declared my gratitudes as if they were already part of my daily life...and then to my surprise, I realized I was manifesting everything I was putting out there. I am known for running pretty high on the positivity scale and when you choose to embrace a more positive outlook, you create a higher energetic frequency. Be mindful of your positive thoughts and acknowledge how they make you feel.

Now I know you have all heard about the importance of being grateful etc., but I took this to a new level, and you can too. It takes clarity and being specific about what you know you want and what you do not. The Universe will deliver but you better be clear on what you are asking for. Some suggestions I focused on were being grateful for my healthy body and immune system; grateful for money and opportunities from expected and unexpected places; grateful for my safe living space for me and Lucy. We all have so much to be grateful for when you flip your focus.

Intentions are powerful. I set an intention at the beginning of each day after I list my gratitudes. If daily seems overwhelming, start with **one** thing to commit to per week and focus on it, repeating it daily. When you are stating your intention say it as if it has already happened and you are living it.

Here is the difference that I experienced that changed my life. You can say all the affirmations and gratitude statements that you want, but if you do not make the necessary changes to bring it to fruition, it's not going to happen.

For example, when I look back at all of my years of notes in programs learning to work with horses and help others tune in, my affirmations are the same. "I am at my ideal weight and look good in my clothes." That was a repeated one through the years. What I was not being as intentional about, was taking action and making the necessary positive changes.

Remember, where your focus goes, energy flows, so focus on what you DO want to manifest. This is truly intentional living.

Who's in Your First-Class Cabin?

One of my favorite sayings is *"Who's in your First-Class Cabin?"* We hold the boarding passes for the coveted space for the select few and should only let those people board that encourage us to become our best selves, not those who try to deplete our energy. Our overall well-being and mindset have a lot to do with the people we choose to allow into our personal space and spend the most time with.

As an empath, I physically feel people's energy especially those who are a great fit as well as those who are NOT and are inauthentic. In some cases, you can easily choose not to be around them, and sometimes it is not so easy if you are working with them. So, you find a way to protect your energy and catch yourself before you get triggered. This is not always easy, but acknowledging it is the first step.

As we have been told, if you are triggered by someone's behavior it may be reflecting behavior that you possess so it is a good wake-up call to pay attention to the root cause. Again, this is a reality check and a learning experience for you to choose to act differently.

Family members can be a big trigger for many of us. Our families can be a major source of stress and energy depletion. They are the ones who created the buttons they push and have years of experience. It is your choice to decide if you wish to participate in the drama, or not to feed into it and protect your energy.

Start to notice how you feel when you are around people that you spend the most time with. Do they inspire you and encourage you to be your best self, or do they deplete your energy, dwell in the negatives, and leave you feeling drained after spending time with them? When you surround yourself with negativity both in thought and physically, it can make you sick. Your circle is your choice, and your First-Class Cabin should be reserved for a select few.

Remember, the people you surround yourself with will have a great impact on your ability to embrace your best self. Raise the bar for your circle if those individuals in your circle of people do not inspire you.

Once you begin a regular practice of catching yourself starting to get snarky or negative, take a breath and feel into that. Do not deflect your inner funk on others, breathe into it, and give yourself a break. Flip the script and focus on some positives and you will feel an immediate lightness vs. the heaviness that comes with living in a negative and judgmental space. Try it...it works!

Permission to Dance in the Moment

When you live in a constant state of stress, EVERYTHING can get to you. The slightest thing can piss you off. What I realized when I intentionally made these positive changes and committed to taking the necessary action each day, was that I truly did feel different. Almost lighter. Yes, literally as I had lost 20 pounds, but just overall. I had a new appreciation for slowing down and noticing and appreciating the little things. We all have this ability, yet we sometimes allow ourselves to get so wrapped up in the drama, social media, blah blah blah. Turn it off. The only way you can truly tune in is to turn it off!

Life happens and we all are on our journey. We have a choice to react or respond when things happen that are outside of our control. When we choose to dance in the moment and go with the flow the situation doesn't seem so overwhelming. We have all heard the term "go with the flow" and it originated from going with the flow of the river. When you visualize that meaning, does it make sense to try to paddle upstream of a raging river? Uh, no. So next time life happens to you, take a breath, ask if this is within your control or not, and then dance in the moment and direct your energy to the most positive outcome possible. Just by shifting your energy around it, you can help direct the possibilities for more positivity.

Lessons from My Horses

Vanity's Mountain Genius, aka Dooby

Dooby taught me empathy, patience, love, heart-ache. He had been donated to the equestrian college due to a rigorous show training program that blew his mind. He wasn't an easy horse, so he wasn't a good fit for the college. As a young horse-crazy teen, I fell in love and just connected with him as a horse, not as a well-bred show animal with no feelings. He was my first love and first broken heart. My regret, and possibly something I've yet to process, is that I couldn't explain to him why he had to go to a new home and give him a proper goodbye. I built a wall, walked away, and never followed up with his new owners or life.

Impressively Sassy aka Sassy

Sassy was my first horse after my 16-year self-imposed break from anything horse-related. She was a beautiful mare with ice blue eyes against her dark liver chestnut coat with a wide white stripe on her face. She and her owner didn't get along so the trainers at the barn let me try her out and we just clicked. We were true partners and became the team to beat competitively in the National Paint Horse show circuit.

She was a kind mare, unlike many mares that make no bones about where you stand with them. Sassy taught me how to embrace the horses again as well as one of the most important lessons of presence. You cannot have your own agenda or be thinking about something else when you are riding. The horses will remind you quickly that you better get your head back in the arena!

Invitation Nowhere, aka Romeo

Romeo was my soul horse. Possibly one of the most beautiful horses I have ever seen, but his heart, oh his huge heart is what bound us together. I could write a love story about Romeo, but here are the basics...I bought Romeo when I was progressing with my horse show career and needed a more competitive horse for the Quarter Horse circuit. He was WAAY out of my price range and a stallion, but my trainer encouraged me to try him out. It was love at first ride and somehow, I figured out how to pull the money together to buy him. He cost more than my luxury car at the time, but I HAD to have him. He had a condition known as sarcoids that pretty much sidelined our show career early on and resulted in astronomical vet bills, but through it all, he was the picture of resilience, patience, and love. After I departed from my corporate life, Romeo and Sassy were my equine business partners in Unbridle It.

I sent Romeo to Colorado to be used in an equine coaching program that I was participating in, and he soon became the favorite that everyone wanted to work with. I learned from that experience the importance of prioritizing and honoring horses that are used for any type of therapy as they can experience their own trauma if not allowed to be turned out to run, kick and roll to get rid of the human energy that they are subjected to. It was not intentional, but unfortunately, the experience had an impact on his already compromised immune system and terminal condition. Part of my mission is to be a voice for the horses to ensure practitioners are always honoring the horses that are used in equine therapy and coaching practices. There is so much healing to be done for the humans, and we must make sure we are honoring our horses first.

For more details about my journey with the horses and how that helped strengthen my resilience, please visit my website www.unbridleit.com for a FREE Ebook, *Unbridle Your Passion and Lead with Your Heart,* as featured in the Amazon bestselling book, *From Resilience to Brilliance.*

MY NOTES – BOSSMARE'S TIPS FROM THE TRAIL

MEET THE AUTHOR
Leeanne Gardner aka "Bossmare"

A lifelong love of horses resulted in profound life lessons for Leeanne, including the importance of authenticity, the power of presence, the necessity of perseverance, and the value of resilience.

During her successful twenty-five-year corporate career in technology and luxury hospitality, she discovered that many of her colleagues couldn't answer the question, "What lights you up?" Through her connection with horses, Leeanne learned the significance for each of us to embrace our passion as well as have a balance between our business and personal life.

Upon her departure from the corporate world

in 2008, she created *Unbridle It, LLC* partnering with her beloved horses Sassy and Romeo. The original mission was to help people tap into their true potential or a long-lost passion to find more life fulfillment through working with the horses.

However, it quickly became apparent that many purpose-driven companies also needed to express their passion and values and could use Leeanne's extensive business skills to help with their marketing, branding, and events.

In March of 2020, just as the Coronavirus pandemic was taking hold of the world, Leeanne felt a sense of excitement and was inspired to take the reins and transform all aspects of her life. She felt like she was personally and professionally out of alignment and therefore she was unhappy.

She saw the pandemic as a major RESET button and an opportunity for a positive life transformation not only for herself but also for individuals and businesses who were ready to step up and embrace the changes that needed to occur so they too could "create their happy."

Upon the suggestion of many friends who witnessed Leeanne's transformation, she compiled her journey and is sharing her roadmap to positive change in *Unbridle It! Buck Up and Create Your Happy*.

As she says, *"You'll never know your full potential until you Unbridle It!"*

If you would like to discuss speaking opportunities for Leeanne to deliver motivational and energizing presentations to your group, or if you would like to learn more about how to work with her please visit:

www.Unbridleit.com

or email her at:

Bossmare@Unbridleit.com

Let's Stay Connected!

Sign up for the email list for access to full-sized worksheets, tips, upcoming events, and more! Visit www.unbridleit.com

Facebook – @Unbridleit

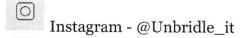 Instagram - @Unbridle_it

 LinkedIn – leeannegardneraz

ACKNOWLEDGMENTS

I'd like to acknowledge these Major contributors to my journey from the fixtures in my First-Class Cabin.

Susan F. Moody, anything business support related, including pulling together this book.
www.MzBizWiz.com

Elizabeth Summers, esoteric numerologist and medium who provides amazing and accurate insights.
www.ElizabethSummers.com

Karen M. Winkelman, great friend, incredible intuitive and numerologist.
www.thelifecraftingguide.com